Prime Time Writers

Writing from the Women
at Emmanuel Baptist Church

Spring 2011

D1521285

NY Writers Coalition Press

Editor: Shaina Feinberg
Layout: Deborah Clearman
Cover and Interior Art: Mildred Park

Prime Time Writers contains writing by the members of creative writing workshops for participants in the Prime Time Ministry conducted by NY Writers Coalition Inc. at the Emmanuel Baptist Church.

NY Writers Coalition thanks the following supporters, without whom this writing workshop and anthology would not exist: Brooklyn Community Foundation, Emmanuel Baptist Church, Kalliopeia Foundation, NYC Department of Cultural Affairs, NYC Council Member Latitia James, State Senator Velmanette Montgomery, Two West Foundation, the WellMet Group, and all our individual donors and attendees of our annual Write-A-Thon.

NY Writers Coalition Inc. is a not-for-profit organization that provides free creative writing workshops throughout New York City for people from groups that have been historically deprived of voice in our society. For more information about NY Writers Coalition Inc.:

NY Writers Coalition Inc.
80 Hanson Place #603
Brooklyn, NY 11217
718-398-2883
info@nywriterscoalition.org
www.nywriterscoalition.org

Prime Time Ministry is an intentional ministry designed by, with, and for adults 50 and over in our church and community. It seeks to promote the well being of all its members in areas affecting their physical, socioeconomic, and spiritual needs. **Emmanuel Baptist Church**, located in the Ft. Greene/Clinton Hill section of Brooklyn, provides contemporary and dynamic Christian teaching, preaching and discipleship development to an intergenerational congregation of approximately 4,000.

Emmanuel Baptist Church
279 Lafayette Avenue
Brooklyn, NY 11238
718-622-1107
www.ebc-ny.org

INTRODUCTION

Jean Hill came in a little late wearing an orange t-shirt with festive orange fringes dangling front, back and center, as well as off the sleeves. I asked her how she was doing and she muttered a faint reply. Somewhere between OK and hot and tired. She saddled into her chair and I leaned over to her and whispered. "We're writing about lemons," I said, pointing at the slice of lemon that was on the desk in front of her chair.

"Lemons?!" Jean did nothing to hide her dislike of the topic I had chosen.

"Uh, well, I mean, we're letting the smell of lemons bring us back."

"Back to lemons?"

I shrugged. Jean furrowed her brow, pulled out a piece of paper and a pen and started to write. Since I began facilitating the Prime Time workshop at the Emmanuel Baptist Church, over a year ago, only a few of the dozens of exercises I've presented have not been met with this same kind of sentiment: *Lemons?! Are you kidding me? I hate lemons!*

Once I made the mistake of asking the ladies to write about having an enemy over for dinner. *An enemy? My enemy? What? I don't have an enemy! You think I have an enemy? If I did have an enemy I wouldn't be having him or her over for dinner.* Eventually, everyone got to writing.

Yes, it is true that weekly someone would protest loudly or roll their eyes or cross their arms over their chests and let out a little *hmmmph*. But weekly these ladies would saddle up their reluctant horses and ride off, slowly at first, and then more quickly, into the sunset for fifteen to twenty minutes, bringing back with them the most wonderful stories—true or imagined. Full of life and color and characters sometimes so hilarious we were all in tears laughing.

So, ladies, go on. Protest, dear friends. Grumble as much as you like, because if there has ever been a group of women who, when given lemons can make lemonade, it is you. The women of Prime Time. And I am so lucky to be a witness to it every week.

Shaina Feinberg, Workshop Leader
February, 2011

ELIZABETH CARR

BE THE LIGHT
In remembrance of Catherine

December 17, 2009, arrived bright and crisp. It was one of those gorgeous New York days with just enough bite in the air to make you bundle up and step lively! The Prime Timers stepped quickly into the interior of Junior's Restaurant. The familiar setting was not fancy, but it was warm and comfortable. There were twelve of us, a significant number as followers of Christ. We spread out in the corner booth and perused the luncheon menu, chatting and exchanging thoughts. I sat at the end of the table closest to the door, while Catherine sat at the far end of the table. Had I known how events would unfold, I would have moved closer or mingled more, like we do at office parties. We all would have listened more intently to the music of her voice. We had no inkling that the music would stop so abruptly.

We were twelve women, laughing, celebrating the holidays to come. Twelve women in December saluting our writing class facilitator. Twelve women; and one would never return to her home with family, friends, furnishings and Christmas goodies waiting for her.

When leaving Junior's, Catherine turned, gave me a hug, and smilingly said, "You are a ray of sunshine!" Her words made me glow and I received them like a wonderful surprise gift, and with a sense of communion. This mother, grandmother and friend to all, validated what love is.

Shortly after lunch on her way home she became ill, and was rushed to the hospital by angels put there for a purpose.

Within a few days Catherine Copney went to her own bright mansion.

Her vivid stories, her warm smile and soft, sweet voice always gave off rays of sunshine. It made you feel you were in the sunlight of her love. Made you feel that *you and I* might be the light!

LIFE AND LEMONS

Lemons have a special appeal to me. The lemon engages all my senses: its egg-like shape fits perfectly in the hand, as snug as a glove; the bright yellow color catches the eye and the smell of it—crisp and citric—is easy "aromatherapy on the run."

When its juices are extracted, it's the pure lemon flavor we get, not an imitation!

That flavor is the bottled memory of the Watkins Man who went house to house in days of old, selling first to my Grandma Carrie whose lemon cake and frosting would make our mouths water then smile with undiluted pleasure. Her passel of grandkids waited impatiently on the porch to get the spoon to lick, or a bite of her "tester" cake to make sure it was good enough. To me, it was always good enough!

Then and now, lemon cake is my #1 favorite.

Later, my Mother made her lemon cakes with jelly in the middle, combining vanilla and lemon flavors bought from the same Watkins man until he retired... or maybe went out of business from modern supermarket products. Yet, today the taste of homemade lemon cake is embedded deep in my psyche and in my soul.

I learned that the yellow lemon also serves a variety

of functions: Stuffed into a whole chicken, it helps to keep the bird moist and tasty. It's a must with seafood. It can lighten skin and blemishes, even dusky knees if applied diligently. Lemon Pledge furniture polish is a household staple that wears down my natural avoidance of housework—it's so fresh! Even water tastes better with a slice.

In perfumes and soaps, the sharp and sweet citric aroma is a perfect combination to outdoor sports and activities that demand a sharp mind and quick reactions for a sweet outcome.

But, the childhood pleasure I recall most vividly is sneaking cups of precious sugar and making lemonade after the grown ups went to work or went downtown. I remember sitting on the steps or in a tire swing with friends, swinging our legs and feeling content with the world, enjoying life in its simplest form.

To quote Langston Hughes, "Life for me ain't been no crystal stair." But I believe that *when life gives you lemons, making lemonade* can quench your thirst and give you pleasure to hold you for a little while.

THE PERFECT GIFT

I was twenty years old and had moved out on my own to a kitchenette on Madison Avenue! Okay, it was Madison Avenue, Brooklyn, but I was still "moving on up."

My boyfriend Ronnie visited me there often and he had begun to talk about what he wanted for his birthday in July. He was clear that he did not want a store-bought present.

It was getting harder to deny him as I looked into his dark brown eyes set in chiseled Creole features, completed by a long, lean body that reflected the discipline of his military training. It didn't help that his voice was like warm molasses. When he spoke in his Louisiana drawl, it poured over me like I was a stack of pancakes! So, finally, my defenses and judgment crumbled and I said, "Yes, I'll do what you want."

The day before his birthday was Saturday and he was at my door, real early, making sure that I didn't forget. Then, whistling a happy tune, off he went to the drugstore to pick up what was needed. Meanwhile, I started warming water and taking out a towel and putting aside the Vaseline as a standby. I was nervous, feeling jittery.

Ronnie returned full of smiles and commenced to get ready, slowly taking out the articles he bought: potatoes, rubber gloves, a comb, and Red Devil lye. He showed me what to do and then gave me a big hug as he sat down in my only chair. He was ready. I closed my eyes, hoping for courage.

First, I put the towel around his shoulders: next I rubbed the Vaseline on his scalp, then with a wooden spoon, spread the bubbling mixture of potato and lye on his head of tight curls. My eyes were tearing from the fumes—and from the loss of those soft curls I loved to touch.

After fifteen or twenty minutes, he surrendered; he couldn't take the burn anymore. I dipped his head in cool water then washed it in warm water and patted it dry. When I was done, I handed him the mirror.

Although his face was still twitching from that burning lye, Ronnie broke into a smile that lit up the little room. Wow! He now had straight hair just like Jackie Wilson, The Temptations, and other entertainers of the day.

He pronounced: "Baby, this is the best gift you could ever give me! Thank You!!"

For him, it was the perfect gift; for me, it was a test of devotion, not just a notion.

LETTER TO BROOKLYN

Dear Brooklyn,

Moving here many years ago was not a happy experience, even though I was a newlywed. It was huge and a little frightening. There were so many buildings, and besides, Virginia was where I wanted to be. That's where I knew everyone in my neighborhood by name and children could freely run in and out of doors to play. That's where the grass was green and soft between my toes. Virginia trees were tall and full and everywhere you looked were flowers of many colors.

Yes, that was then. Now, after many years in Brooklyn, I have grown accustomed to my adopted home. I enjoy your many attributes—the beautiful parks where the green grass sprouts, the tall trees and colorful flowers, too. The architecture is unbelievably precise—from historic to super modern.

Corn beef, pastrami, salami and cheeses galore really give my palate such unbelievable pleasure. Italian dishes are my favorite and a slice of pizza tops it all. Bagels and cream cheese and delicious pastries from various neighborhoods really make Brooklyn so unique.

Well, Brooklyn, I thought you might want to know that I now see your true personality, character and beauty and I love you very much. There is no other place like you!

Sincerely,
A transplanted Brooklynite

P.S. I am thinking of moving back to Virginia—one day.

NEAL'S VEGETABLE GARDEN

As a child, I remember that my father always had a garden in our large back yard in Norfolk, Virginia. Corn on the cob, collard greens, cucumbers, string beans, potatoes, tomatoes, butter beans and tiny watermelons grew there. My father really wanted to be a farmer, I believe, and this was his passion.

Alveta, Yvonne and I had fun picking and shelling the butter beans. Then we would put them in quart-size baskets and my mother sold them, canned some for the winter months, and gave some away to the family. We ate well and had a plenty.

From time to time, I would see my father sitting in the garden on his little stool. He would stay for a long time just taking in the earth and all around him seeming very peaceful. I would laugh and say to him, "Hey Daddy, Daddy, how does your garden grow?" Or, "Daddy, are you watching your garden grow?" He would smile. That certainly was the way it seemed to me.

Even years later, when all of us had left home, he still planted, and he was in his eighties, on into his nineties. All that he grew then he gave to all the neighbors. At ninety-five he died. I think we could have buried him right there in his garden if that had been allowed.

I LOVE MY JOB

Never in my wildest dreams could I have imagined that I would become the education director of a daycare center during my retirement years at sixty plus. Yet, that is exactly what happened. After I retired, I had a couple of tutoring and part-time teaching positions and that was good. There was still plenty of time for fun and relaxation and all the things retirees do. Then along came the offer for this full-time director position. I hesitated in making a decision for a while and stalled in meeting with the powers that be, because I wasn't sure I wanted to lock up all of my free post-employment time. That was back in 2004, and I am still there. Well, so much for agreeing at the outset to stay for two years. So began my second career.

My days are busy and full of activity, from early morning to parents' quitting time. I have no regrets and I find that I am having fun, too. Thank God Emmanuel has so many Prime Time happenings right here at the church. I am involved in the exercise class, Tai Chi, creative writing, and the small group experience. How, do I do this? Well, I do have a lunch hour.

Nothing pleases me more than my daily morning greeting to the children, "Good morning boys and girls," and their response, "Good morning Ms. Clarke."

What a way to start the day, and this brings a smile to my heart. I call these little ones "my beautiful children" and they truly are. What happens when they are pre-teens and teens, I do not know. But now they are little angels—most of the time. When prospective parents come to our center for a tour, upon entering the classroom, I say to them these are our beautiful children. They are smart, curious, spontaneous, and gifted. A few years back, there was a show called "Kids Say the Darndest Things." That is a fact, and whatever they say are their original thoughts.

What can I say? I traded my free time for a full time job with two-, three-, four-, and five-year-olds, and I love my job.

JEAN HILL

GUILTY PLEASURES

Last week I went on a fitness retreat up to Ellen-ville, New York. I was glad that I went because I have entered the health challenge at the church. I have been doing well. As we got to the hotel, I was expecting lunch to be served. Instead, we had a table full of Danishes, brownies, etc. I knew I shouldn't but I did eat some. Would you believe, later they brought out a big bowl of fruit. I went up and got two cups of fruit. I did get to walk a little before dinner. It was buffet and I really went to town, saying to myself I only live once. Knowing I will be eating things I normally don't now. Steak, shrimps, mashed potatoes, etc. Plus a slice of cheesecake. For breakfast the next day: French toast, eggs, home fries, pork sausages, fruit rolls. Now my conscience is really bothering me. Before lunch we had an exercise class. I really needed it. Lunch: rib, rice, vegetable, fried chicken, bread. This time I didn't have dessert. While coming home I started thinking of the weekend. It was my guilty pleasure. I have been doing much better since I'm back home and my health challenge is doing well.

MY FEET

Let me tell you about my feet. At times I have to use my cane. I have my good days and bad ones. Everybody knows I love to dance. There isn't a dance I don't do including hip hop. I was talking to Pastor Hayes one day and I told him about how I can't walk, but I can dance. He got so tickled at what I said. He has seen me praise dance in the church. One day I was trying to get up on the bus, having a hard time. I looked at the bus driver and said I need some new legs and feet. He just smiled. He told me to take my time.

Catherine, who is no longer with us, asked me to come upstairs to her apartment. She handed me a package. She had just gotten back from Atlanta. I opened it and it was a plaque which said, "If you can talk, you can sing," (not me) "If you can walk you can dance." That's me. I now have it in my wall unit. It's a reminder of what a beautiful person she was. We all miss her.

MAKING SOMETHING OUT OF NOTHING

Children can always be counted on to make something out of nothing. I can remember as a child, playing in the area of Norfolk, Virginia, called Rosemount, with the children of the neighborhood.

There was a semi-forested area in the back of my house that we would pretend was a jungle.

Yes, we would march to the jungle daily and pretend to see ferocious animals and beasts. Sticks became swords, bows and arrows, and clubs. Little streams of water became raging rivers.

Oh, the fun we had each day.

Sometimes, we would pack a lunch of peanut butter sandwiches and go off into the "jungle" with our meager provisions for an extended adventure.

Once, we came to the edge of the "forest" and peeked into "forbidden land." Beautiful homes came into view with people who looked unlike us. A cry rang out. "They saw us. Run!"

With fear in each breast, we traversed the raging river, the huge fallen trunks of trees to safely land in "friendly territory."

Yes, we kids had many an adventure—inventing playtime with nothing but our vivid imaginations.

BEATRICE JACKSON

BAGS THAT RELEASE MEMORIES

I am sort of a pack rat when it comes to mail and almost everything else. My "computer room" in the back kitchen was the place relegated to my stash of papers and mail.

I have resigned myself to clean up this growing room of. . .must I say, "trash?"

I try to take out one or two bags a day. Sometimes I reach my goal and some days—not. I go through each piece of mail and paper, either shredding or putting aside to be saved.

This morning, as I went through my most recent bag, I came across three pictures. Two were of my first Tiger Cub group with my four-year-old grandson holding up the paper snakes we had made.

I smiled as I remembered how some days, it would just be me and him for that hour of working and playing together. We always played a board game (Candy Land) until the other Tiger Cubs arrived.

I'm not sure who enjoyed those times together more—me or him.

In the back of my mind I said, "Today, Jair is ten years old and this may be his last birthday I will see him celebrate in Brooklyn." My daughter is building a house in Charlotte.

The third picture was of my new-found father, with my sister and her son. Yes, I smiled as I laid the three pictures aside to be saved. Getting rid of my clutter can still give me some joy.

Symbolic Object from Childhood

How can I ever forget that fateful Friday evening a number of years past, when the phone rang and Mama was on the line telling me my best friend ever had died suddenly? I dropped the phone like the falling of my heart upon hearing this sad news. I could not conceive her death. Wasn't it just a few weeks back that I had seen her when I visited my home where the two of us had grown up? She was looking so healthy and well, and was wearing the most gorgeous green dress I had ever seen. She was together; in sync with herself as if she waved with the wind.

I shall never forget when Melody and I first met; maybe I should say when I became cognizant of her. I had seen her all along but had not paid too much attention to her. I know she had seen me also. She wasn't the pushy type! Then one day I started talking to her and knew she was listening intensely to everything I said without making comments. Mama had always told me when I was a little girl to pick my friends with care. "Everyone is not your friend. In fact, true friends are few and far between," she said.

Somehow when I met Melody, I knew I could trust her. First I told her a secret just to test her. As time passed and no one else repeated what I told Melody, I knew for sure I could trust her; that she would keep my secrets and always had my back.

She never laughed at me like some of my other friends when I said silly things. Melody would simply nod her head into the wind in agreement.

When I came back to the telephone I was surprised that Mama was still holding on. "What did she die from Mama?"

"Well honey," she sighed, "she was killed by a bolt of lightning. It struck and tumbled her over. We mourned her demise. **Your cherry tree Melody is dead!!!**"

DEVASTATED

I'm writing on a subject most people will not discuss. But I hope that it will help others.

Last year around this time I was in the hospital. I went to get a secondary X-ray of my lungs, following up from an X-ray I took in December, 2009.

You see, I had already been diagnosed with what is called COPD, Chronic Obstructive Pulmonary Disease/Disorder. I'm on oxygen 24/7 and suffer from SOB, shortness of breath, as a result of COPD. I am well with all of that—taking medications, pacing myself and getting the rest I need.

While in the hospital after the X-rays that resulted, the doctors ordered what is called a Cat Scan. It wasn't until the results of the Cat Scan that the doctors diagnosed me with cancer of the left lung; plus I had a collapsed lung and fluid too.

I was DEVASTATED. If it looks like I was screaming, using all capitals, yes I was screaming. I was DEVASTATED, ANGRY, and highly UPSET. Why? Because I was in and out of the hospital and took several X-rays and never once was given the diagnosis of cancer. When I think back, way back, I feel it wasn't time for me to know. I'm going to be honest about it: I spent two, three days planning my funeral, having a real pity party. After the tears. Then it was like DING. . . . like someone slapped you in the back of the head to get you to remember something that you already knew and bring it to the front of your mind: Jesus. Jesus said, "By my stripes I healed all sickness, illness, and diseases."

I gave my cancer to God; the very moment I did that it was like weights, very heavy weights, were lifted off my shoulders. Now I'm well with that too.

There is a song that we sing in Emmanuel Baptist Church, "Give it all to Him, Give it to God in prayer."

Because of my COPD surgery was not an option. I began chemo in February, 2010, and continued until December, 2010.

My doctor ordered a Pet Scan to find out if any cancer spread to any other part of my body. If it did, I would have to either go back to chemo or start radiation therapy. The results of the Pet Scan: there was no spreading of cancer in the body. The doctor took me off the chemo and in two months I take another Pet Scan. I'm happy that my body is taking a break from chemo because chemo side effects are rough on the body. I'm not exactly out of the woods, if you know what I mean, but I feel great.

I want to praise God for all my blessings. Some may think that I'm krazy because I'm blessed. So what. I'm krazy. I spell it with a *k*—krazy. I also thank my spiritual family for all that you did for me. I need not to mention names because you already know who you are. All the prayers, lots and lots of prayers, visits, get well cards, and gifts—and more, the love I received. I also thank my biological family who accompanied me to chemo treatments for eleven months. They just would not let me go to chemo without them. Each member took turns going with me.

So my devastation turned out to be a Testimony meant to help others. One of my prayers is that there will be a cure for all kinds of cancer and that it will be available to all men, women, boys, and girls without cost. Can't have a testimony without going through the test.

I wasn't going to go here but I must: if you smoke, stop. My support group calls it Sickaretts. They make you sick and beyond. That's another one of my prayers. "We discover our role in life through our relationships with God and others."

Thank You Lord.

JAQUELINE MURRAY

HEALTHY LIFE

At this stage of my life, my mind is usually focused on my health.

Which doctor's appointment is today: which procedure is scheduled for next week? What foods can I eat, does this have too much salt?

Do I have enough energy to make it downtown to the movies?

Times have really changed; body parts don't seem to react the way they once did. When I bend over I may not find it so easy to get back up. When I place something down I may not remember where. The pills of all colors and descriptions that have become a part of my daily routine, I have difficulty remembering if I took them or not.

My latest fear is that I hope the pills remember where to go: the blue one to the head, the white one to the stomach, and the little red one to the left knee.

SNOW

Maggie hated snow storms. She didn't like getting her feet wet. She hated putting on that long, heavy coat; it was tight and restricted her movements.

She hated getting her hair wet, all full of that white stuff, only to look like something the cat dragged in.

Maggie in fact hated the winter; it was cold and windy.

It was so nice to remain inside where it was cozy and warm. It was fun to look out of the window and watch others all bundled up against the winds, braving the elements. It was great to enjoy a delicious meal and then cuddle up and take a nap on the couch.

Every time Maggie saw Nick reach for the leash and say, "Come on girl!" she hid under the bed.

Oh for the joy of summer.

JAQUELINE MURRAY

I NEVER NOTICED

A few years ago everything was going well. The cute young thing in the mirror was walking to work. Everything stood upright, chewed her steak with a full set of teeth and did a mean electric slide on the dance floor.

One day after stepping on a bus, a young girl jumped up out of her seat, and with a smile said, "You can have my seat, Ma'am." Well, that really knocked my socks off. Was she speaking to me? I said as I elbowed the little girl in front of me out of the way and plopped down. My mind wandered; why did she give me a seat? Did I look old?

I went straight home and looked closely in the full length mirror.

Well, I'll be darned, where did that gray hair come from? How long have these smile lines been etched in my face? I turned sideways. My boobs were busy listening to my growling stomach. I looked down and couldn't see my feet, a big roll was in the way.

In the rear a large bump had replaced my once cute booty. I slowly limped away from the mirror. Hey old girl, I hardly know you; when did this happen?

DEAR BROOKLYN

This is a belated love letter to a place that's been my home for most of my long life. When I returned to New York City in 1952, you welcomed me. I heard cheering Brooklyn Dodgers fans who had won another pennant and as a newcomer, I asked, "Why are they so excited?"

I became a jubilant Dodger fan later and spent many afternoons yelling in Ebbets Field bleachers for Jackie Robinson and Roy Campanella. Even when I deserted you for Manhattan and the Bronx I still visited friends for parties and other festivities. Coney Island and the Cyclone Roller Coaster were one of my early habitats, and the Empire Rollerdome witnessed many knee and elbow scrapes from falls as I tried to skate. Central Park was replaced by Prospect Park when I returned to Brooklyn in 1960. And I've spent much more time at the Grand Army Plaza branch library than the 42nd Street one. You are where I entered college at Brooklyn College after a long subway ride to the end of the line. Fulton Street replaced Lenox Avenue and I found a job on Jay Street instead of Park Row. Buses replaced subways for my daily commute. Flatbush, Crown Heights, Park Slope, Fort

Greene and Clinton Hill all housed me. Bedford Stuyvesant, Carroll Gardens, Brownsville and many others have sheltered and entertained my friends, family and co-workers. I miss you when I leave you, complain about the high rise buildings being erected which change your small town residential appearance, but realize that change is necessary. We can find all kinds of ethnic foods in our supermarkets and neighborhood restaurants. We're not required to travel far to visit the world. It's at our doorstep or stoop. Cosmo Brooklyn, that's you.

MILDRED PARK

DREAM, DREAM, DREAM

As long as my mind works, I'll dream. I was a fanciful child, loving stories of once upon a time, they lived happily ever after, and I still prefer happy endings to gruesome dramas. As a crafter, I'm always thinking of my next project, waiting for my next vacation, remembering the previous. I can't imagine not dreaming of what to see, where to go, who'll be there, what to wear, what to cook and eat, what to plant on my terrace, waiting for the seed or plant to grow, bloom or fruit. Seeing the babies turn into toddlers, adolescents, and hopefully adults through many generations. What to read, watch on TV, see on stage. I call myself a recycled teenager; sometimes I'm even younger and I love Peter Pan's song, "I Won't Grow Up." Maturity has its perks but youth should have dreams and I'll hold onto mine. Replace one done with one yet to happen, but still keeping something to look forward to. See each new day as a promise, a present, a gift to be opened.

Keep the dream alive; I have a dream. Some of our leaders encouraged us to keep striving for a better tomorrow. And I hope to do just that. With my eyes wide open, I'm dreaming. So many popular songs

INSTRUCTION MANUAL

Speak clearly when asking or informing. Don't yell or scream; smile only if genuine. Be definite, not wishy-washy. Only give information that's repeatable. I'm not a secret keeper; things spill out all the time. Have instructions in printed form with clear illustrations and charts. I'm literate. I can stay for the long haul if conditions are to my liking, but will not hesitate to quit when disappointed. I play by the rules of games, don't like cheating or cheaters. Am not a gambler unless the odds are all in my favor. Expect to be paid what I am worth and am owed and on time. If not, don't expect a second chance. Give people the benefit of the doubt until I learn they're not to be believed or trusted. Don't spend much time crying, prefer to laugh. Am punctual and reliable, expect others to be the same. If I say I will, you can rely on that unless unavoidable things like illness or weather prevent me from accomplishing. You can expect a good day's work for the salary and may enjoy the process also. Prefer accuracy to speed.

WHEN I GROW TOO OLD TO DREAM I'LL HAVE YOU TO REMEMBER

Oh, I remember it well, the day we met at the Jazz Festival in Wilmington, Delaware. I was on a long business trip from Chicago for eight weeks and you lived in Philadelphia, Pennsylvania. We shared many experiences for the next eight years.

I remember the intimate moments and dinners at the Hotel DuPont. You never allowed me to use my expense account or personal money when we were together. I always laughed as you dared me to open your car door to go in or out. You always preferred me dressed in suits and looking into your eyes.

Your heart and hugs were warm. You were proud of my accomplishments at work and how supportive I was of my daughter. I admired all of the young people you mentored when you taught high school and law school. Gee, you were such a tiger in the Courtroom defending your clients with such zeal and you always made me feel proud.

Remember when we put your Dad's medicine in his applesauce as he smiled at me. I remember when I had Thanksgiving with your family in Connecticut and it was the first time I ate West Indian cuisine. Everyone laughed at my facial expressions. The food was delicious.

I remember when we went to jazz clubs in Philly, Wilmington and Boston and held hands. Yes, we were one. Wow, we had some awesome road trips and our ventures to the petting zoo, to Amish Country, the science store, and eating in Dutch Country.

Oh, mon ami, we spoke the French language to each other. Years later after I got married, we laughed and we even danced with my husband's permission. Yes, we shared so much fun and life's challenges in love. Even today, you are so proud of my daughter.

We had lots of fun. You are a gentlemen, you are handsome, a great scholar, a great son and brother, a great mentor and a friend for life.

OH, I REMEMBER IT WELL!!!

TIME

Now is the time, to understand the time, please let's not waste the time, to study the time and to put time in its place.

What place does time have? Is it eastern, central, everlasting to everlasting, mountain or pacific? Should I sleep away the time or work away time? Must I understand its measure. Or, should I obtain pleasure from the time that God gives to me.

Oh, Lord, thanks for the time to value you and your word. There are years, months, weeks, days, hours, minutes and seconds that humans do not respect. May I value its measure and love its evolution.

Should I blame time for my place in society? Should I SCREAM and PRAY for the major corporations and financial institutions who take advantage of my time. Oh, taxpayers PLEASE bail us out again and again. And yes, as I watch, the people in need wave the flag for America, the Country we LOVE, time after time.

As we beg for wealth to protect the nations, let us beg for wealth to protect our health, fight against crime, homelessness, poverty and build a greater nation, Oh, give PEACE A CHANCE; give peace a chance this time.

Oh, time my time. I cannot wish you speed through my days. I long to hear and experience the tick tock valued by my soul and spirit.

Yes, now is the time to REMEMBER why time is what it is!!!

R.E. SCOTT

MAKING DUE

Taken from "Rhythms of a Black Woman" by R.E. Scott

The black man is our leader, head of household.
But the neck turns the head if the story is told.
Committed to her heritage, her children, her man,
Her brothers and sisters are a part of the plan.
Her skills exploited, she stands like a tower.
It's forever her, the source of our power,
When cupboards are bare and the rent is due,
When money is short, she's got a dollar or two,
Not a sign of worry, not a sign of her fears,
The eyes say courage, no regrets no tears.

Our supper was late but quite fulfilling,
The light bill was due but we looked up at the ceiling
We cannot forget nor fail to respect.
Her song is of faith, no signs of regret.
The body submits, the mind cries out
There is no sorrow, there is no doubt.
When the day is complete, cleaning and shopping
Washing and ironing, cooking and chopping
The head is at ease maxing and relaxing
She's still on her feet mending and waxing.

It's the midnight hour her time for release.
Can she really be free, can she find her peace?
As she unfolds in warm water to enter the glow
Her thoughts are of family and tomorrow's new show.
Her muscles uncurl to the thoughts of our needs.
Her heart beats slower around the rhythm of our pleas
As the stress melts like honey on a warm slice of bread
The whisper of her blessings glow softly in her head.
The children are well and we've seen another day
God is in His heaven and we have a place to stay
So sleep my loves and I will stand guard
Tomorrow is another day and this woman is in charge.

Walking With God

When thinking about what it has meant for me to walk with God I often wonder, why is it referred to as my walk with Him when we are told at the same time to follow in His footsteps. Well, I finally figured it out.

Not long ago I heard Joel Olsteen relate our walk with God to our relationship with our earthly father. God as a loving, caring and protective provider and each of us as one of His many children.

As a child of God it is for me to be obedient. As a child of God I must be respectful and obey His commands without question as I did with my earthly father.

As a child and until his death I knew without a doubt that my dad was there for me. Every child and grandchild that knew him knew that in any crisis, Daddy was there. We knew that Daddy's love was everlasting and unconditional. And so is God's. We knew that Daddy would provide; he brought home the bacon. He would never let us down. Nor will God. Although sickness came and troubles had to be faced we never felt forsaken; we knew Daddy was there. And so is God. We encountered broken hearts from our first, second and sometimes third loves, and where was Daddy?

There to comfort and assure us that he cared and he would always love and be there for us. So is it with God, our Heavenly Father.

So now, then, I ask myself: Why do I at times falter? Although it is not as often these days, there are times when I ask—why; how? Are you there, Lord? I can only give it up to the fact that He, God, has never been a physical being to me personally. You know, like Mr. Rob the handy man, Mr. Bill the man across the street, or my loving Daddy who lived in the house with us.

I know about His son Jesus who visited briefly, but then I have no authentic image of Him. Therefore, that leaves me with faith. It is my faith that I ask my Heavenly Father to strengthen. Faith as I had with my Daddy. Faith to believe in Him in the good and the bad times. Faith to believe in His presence seen or unseen. Faith to believe that because He is God He is everywhere, with, around and within us all at all times.

RUTH G. SMITH

LOOKING FOR A QUIET PLACE

It was early this fall morning I decided to take a walk through the forest, to be alone in a quiet place with nature. But at the beginning of my walk it was anything but quiet.

With the squirrels scampering through the leaves and up and down the bark of the tree trunks, and birds chirping so loudly as they flew back and forth from tree to tree as if they could not make up their minds as to which tree branch they wanted to perch on. It was so noisy, I could not think.

Just as I resolved that there would be no quietness this day, and with disappointment I started to return home, my mind began to focus on a song entitled, "The Blood Will Never Lose Its Power."

To my wonder the sounds around me became melodious. It wasn't noisy anymore. The squirrels scampering through the leaves sounded like the rhythmic shuffle of a snare drum in a band, and the birds chirping as they flew back and forth became sweet music to the song that had entered my head. No, it wasn't the quiet place that I went looking for. It became a harmonious walk with the creator of the leaves for the squirrels to play in, the trees to climb, and the sky for the birds to play in as they made a sweet melody in the air.

A quiet place—no—but a melodious, serene walk in the early morning sun.

RUTH G. SMITH

DON'T GO, DON'T STAY

Don't go if you are not clear on why you are going.

Don't stay if your jellyroll heart is urging you to go.

If you say, I'm your brisk cup of tea when you wake up in the morning. Don't go.

But, if these are just empty words made for flattery just to stroke my ego. Don't stay.

If you wake up in the middle of the night and your restless heart is pounding like the rhythm of the clackity-clack of the train on the track. Don't stay.

You are not the only one confused, because my marshmallow heart tells me to let you go. But I've grown to depend on you to brighten my day with your unblemished smile. I say, "Don't go; stay."

When you lay your head down to sleep you smile at me and say, "Don't go."

But when you fall asleep your subconscious betrays
you in your dreams; you say out loud, "Don't stay."

So I say follow your dreams.

Don't stay.

MAN CAN THAT LADY SING

The first time I heard Billy Holiday sing I was visiting my aunt. She had a large collection of records and Billy Holiday seemed to be her favorite. I'm sure I had heard about her, but I don't remember listening to any of her recordings.

She was probably banned from our radio station. Our radio station played Rhythm and Blues about an hour a day and Jazz was a "no-no." This was in the South many years ago.

As I listened to her sing I thought, she's too whiny for me—this was at age fourteen. I just couldn't understand what all the fuss was about.

As I grew older and life began to knock me about, I learned what it felt like to have the blues. I could feel and understand what Billy Holiday was saying in her songs. Then I began to say about Lady Day, "Man Can That Lady Sing."

ON THE OTHER HAND

When someone says, "But on the other hand," sometimes it could mean they don't know what they believe about the topic or situation, or they don't want to make a commitment either pro or con about said topic or situation.

They may think by not taking a stand they will not offend anyone. They sit on the fence. For instance: A person is asked if they believe that God created the earth. They may answer, "Yes, I believe that there is a higher power that created the earth, but on the other hand there is some evidence of the Big Bang Theory."

Or, do you believe a woman has the right to have an abortion? They may answer, "Yes, I believe a woman has the right to control her own body. But on the other hand, the unborn child has a right to life."

Or, you ask, "Do you agree with those who say red meat can cause cancer or increase our cholesterol level?" They may answer, "Yes, I agree somewhat that red meat is related to those conditions, but on the other hand, red meat is a good source for protein that our bodies need."

The question could be, "Do you totally believe anything?" They may answer "Yes, I do, but on the other hand, I can always change my mind."

My Favorite Item of Clothing Used to Be

My favorite item of clothing used to be a sleeveless, chocolate brown A-line dress made of raffia. We met one lunch hour as I walked down the aisle of a Fifth Avenue retailer. I was browsing when this exotic number adorning the rack beckoned to me. I approached and up close I admired its simple beauty, its crocheted style and the unusual silky straw-like material. I checked the price tag, which read eighty dollars. At the time, the early '70s, this was not within my budget. Reluctantly, I began to walk away but the brown beauty seduced me, whispering, "Try me." I stopped and lingered longingly when suddenly I concluded, what the heck, let's see if it would be as flattering as I had imagined. I grabbed the dress and headed for the fitting room. With anticipation I tried it and when the mirror reflected the desired result, I exclaimed, "Yes!" as I twirled around admiring the fit. It was perfect—sexy, attractive and made for me. I immediately began making plans for the flesh-colored slip I would need to complete the look. I threw the budget to the winds and purchased the brown beauty.

Thus began a love affair with this dress, egged on

by the numerous compliments I received when I wore it. I consider it one of my best purchases. It still resides in my closet today, an item I cannot part with. I hold on to the memory of my introduction to sometimes throwing caution to the winds and not allowing that nagging voice of reason to always rein me in.

IF YOU LIKED IT,
YOU SHOULDA PUT A RING ON IT!

We met one magical evening. The chase was tantalizing. I was wined, dined, complimented, kissed a thousand times and more. I basked in the magic of you, the companionship, the camaraderie, the special feelings, the joy of just seeing you stride into a room. The relationship appeared to be just what I wanted. The joy ride continued for a while, but I began to notice with no seeming destination…no serious discussions, no talk about the future as a couple and lots of evasions when the subject was broached.

It took some time but I finally got the message: this is a fantasy; it is not real.

I am no fool nor am I desperate. No settling for me. Goodbye caught you by surprise. I am not returning your pitiful phone calls nor answering your pathetic emails. You had your chance. "If you liked it, you shoulda put a ring on it."

ROSLYN WILLIAMS

A MOUNTAINTOP EXPERIENCE

I walked into a small chapel in a foreign land—Turkey—with anticipation, since it was purported to be the final home of the Virgin Mary. The line to enter had been long and winding, and as I waited I was unsure of what it contained. The chapel was a small, unimposing brick building. There were no pews. A simple altar with a statue of the Virgin Mary and a few paintings adorning the walls greeted visitors. It was lit by a hundred candles, an exaggeration maybe, but many, anyway. As I approached the altar and lingered to say a brief prayer, a wave of emotion, almost impossible to describe, engulfed me, and I felt as if I were in the presence of something holy and precious, as if the mother of Jesus was greeting me personally and blessing me. I walked out of the chapel weeping and marveling at what may be a once in a lifetime experience.

Made in the USA
Charleston, SC
26 March 2011